AF528451

The Human Machine

Arnold Bennett

Neelkanth Prakashan

ISBN: 978-93-6144-793-8

Publisher: Neelkanth Prakashan

Address: 4760-61, 23, Ansari Road,
Daryaganj, New Delhi-110002
Phone: 9810675061
WhatsApp: +91 9810675061
E-mail: neelkanthprakashan47@gmail.com

Edition: 2024

The Human Machine
Arnold Bennett

Table of Contents

I

TAKING ONESELF FOR GRANTED

There are men who are capable of loving a machine more deeply than they can love a woman. They are among the happiest men on earth. This is not a sneer meanly shot from cover at women. It is simply a statement of notorious fact. Men who worry themselves to distraction over the perfecting of a machine are indubitably blessed beyond their kind. Most of us have known such men. Yesterday they were constructing motorcars. But to-day aeroplanes are in the air—or, at any rate, they ought to be, according to the inventors. Watch the inventors. Invention is not usually their principal business.

They must invent in their spare time. They must invent before breakfast, invent in the Strand between Lyons's and the office, invent after dinner, invent on Sundays. See with what ardour they rush home of a night! See how they seize a half-holiday, like hungry dogs a bone! They don't want golf, bridge, limericks, novels, illustrated magazines, clubs, whisky, starting-prices, hints about neckties, political meetings, yarns, comic songs, anturic salts, nor the smiles that are situate between a gay corsage and a picture hat. They never wonder, at a loss, what they will do next. Their evenings never drag—are always too short. You may, indeed, catch them at twelve o'clock at night on the flat of their backs; but not in bed! No, in a shed, under a machine, holding a candle (whose paths drop fatness) up to the connecting-rod that is strained, or the wheel that is out of centre. They are continually interested, nay, enthralled. They have a machine, and they are perfecting it. They get one part right, and then another goes wrong; and they get that right, and then another goes wrong, and so on. When they are quite sure they have reached perfection, forth issues the machine out of the shed—and in five minutes is smashed up, together with a limb or so of the inventors, just because they had been quite sure too soon. Then the whole business starts again. They do not give up—that particular wreck was, of course, due to a mere oversight; the whole business starts again. For they have glimpsed perfection; they have the gleam of perfection in their souls. Thus their lives run away. 'They will never fly!' you remark, cynically. Well, if they don't? Besides, what about Wright? With all your cynicism, have you never envied them their machine and their passionate interest in it?

You know, perhaps, the moment when, brushing in front of the glass, you detected your first grey hair. You stopped brushing; then you resumed brushing, hastily; you pretended not to be shocked, but you were. Perhaps you know a more disturbing moment than that, the moment when it suddenly occurred to you that you had 'arrived' as far as you ever will arrive; and you had realised as much of your early dream as you ever will realise, and the realisation was utterly unlike the dream; the marriage was excessively prosaic and eternal, not at all what you expected it to be; and your illusions were dissipated; and games and hobbies had an unpleasant core of tedium and futility; and the ideal tobacco-mixture did not exist; and one literary masterpiece resembled another; and all the days that are to come will more or less resemble the present day, until you die; and in an illuminating flash you understood what all those people were driving at when they wrote such unconscionably long letters to the *Telegraph* as to life being worth living or not worth living; and there was naught to be done but face the grey, monotonous future, and pretend to be cheerful with the worm of *ennui* gnawing at your heart! In a word, the moment when it occurred to you that yours is 'the common lot.' In that moment have you not wished—do you not continually wish—for an exhaustless machine, a machine that you could never get to the end of? Would you not give your head to be lying on the flat of your back, peering with a candle, dirty, foiled, catching cold—but absorbed in the pursuit of an object? Have you not gloomily regretted that you were born without a mechanical turn, because there is really something about a machine...?

It has never struck you that you do possess a machine! Oh, blind! Oh, dull! It has never struck you that you have at hand a machine wonderful beyond all mechanisms in sheds, intricate, delicately adjustable, of astounding and miraculous possibilities, interminably interesting! That machine is yourself. 'This fellow is preaching. I won't have it!' you exclaim resentfully. Dear sir, I am not preaching, and, even if I were, I think you *would* have it. I think I can anyhow keep hold of your button for a while, though you pull hard. I am not preaching. I am simply bent on calling your attention to a fact which has perhaps wholly or partially escaped you—namely, that you are the most fascinating bit of machinery that ever was. You do yourself less than justice. It is said that men are only interested in themselves. The truth is that, as a rule, men are interested in every mortal thing except themselves. They have a habit of taking themselves for granted, and that habit is responsible for nine-tenths of the boredom and despair on the face of the planet.

A man will wake up in the middle of the night (usually owing to some form of delightful excess), and his brain will be very active indeed for a space ere he can go to sleep again. In that candid hour, after the exaltation of the evening and before the hope of the dawn, he will see everything in its true colours—except himself. There is nothing like a sleepless couch for a clear vision of one's environment. He will see all his wife's faults and the hopelessness of trying to cure them. He will momentarily see, though with less sharpness of outline, his own faults. He will probably decide that the anxieties of children outweigh the joys connected with children. He will admit all the shortcomings of existence, will face them like a man, grimly, sourly, in a sturdy despair. He will mutter: 'Of course I'm angry! Who wouldn't be? Of course I'm disappointed! Did I expect this twenty years ago? Yes, we ought to save more. But we don't, so there you are! I'm bound to worry! I know I should be better if I didn't smoke so much. I know there's absolutely no sense at all in taking liqueurs. Absurd to be ruffled with her when she's in one of her moods. I don't have enough exercise. Can't be regular, somehow. Not the slightest use hoping that things will be different, because I know they won't. Queer world! Never really what you may call happy, you know. Now, if things were different ...' He loses consciousness.

Observe: he has taken himself for granted, just glancing at his faults and looking away again. It is his environment that has occupied his attention, and his environment—'things'—that he would wish to have 'different,' did he not know, out of the fulness of experience, that it is futile to desire such a change? What he wants is a pipe that won't put itself into his mouth, a glass that won't leap of its own accord to his lips, money that won't slip untouched out of his pocket, legs that without asking will carry him certain miles every day in the open air, habits that practise themselves, a wife that will expand and contract according to his humours, like a Wernicke bookcase, always complete but never finished. Wise man, he perceives at once that he can't have these things. And so he resigns himself to the universe, and settles down to a permanent, restrained discontent. No one shall say he is unreasonable.

You see, he has given no attention to the machine. Let us not call it a flying-machine. Let us call it simply an automobile. There it is on the road, jolting, screeching, rattling, perfuming. And there he is, saying: 'This road ought to be as smooth as velvet. That hill in front is ridiculous, and the descent on the other side positively dangerous. And it's all turns—I can't see a hundred yards in front.' He has a wild idea of trying to force the County Council to sand-paper the road, or of employing the new Territorial Army to remove the hill. But he dismisses that idea—he is so reasonable. He accepts all. He sits clothed in reasonableness on the machine, and accepts all. 'Ass!' you exclaim. 'Why doesn't he get down and inflate that tyre, for one thing? Anyone can see the sparking apparatus is wrong, and it's perfectly certain the gear-box wants oil.

Why doesn't he—?' I will tell you why he doesn't. Just because he isn't aware that he is on a machine at all. He has never examined what he is on. And at the back of his consciousness is a dim idea that he is perched on a piece of solid, immutable rock that runs on castors.

II

AMATEURS IN THE ART OF LIVING

Considering that we have to spend the whole of our lives in this human machine, considering that it is our sole means of contact and compromise with the rest of the world, we really do devote to it very little attention. When I say 'we,' I mean our inmost spirits, the instinctive part, the mystery within that exists. And when I say 'the human machine' I mean the brain and the body—and chiefly the brain. The expression of the soul by means of the brain and body is what we call the art of 'living.' We certainly do not learn this art at school to any appreciable extent. At school we are taught that it is necessary to fling our arms and legs to and fro for so many hours per diem. We are also shown, practically, that our brains are capable of performing certain useful tricks, and that if we do not compel our brains to perform those tricks we shall suffer. Thus one day we run home and proclaim to our delighted parents that eleven twelves are 132. A feat of the brain! So it goes on until our parents begin to look up to us because we can chatter of cosines or sketch the foreign policy of Louis XIV. Good! But not a word about the principles of the art of living yet! Only a few detached rules from our parents, to be blindly followed when particular crises supervene. And, indeed, it would be absurd to talk to a schoolboy about the expression of his soul. He would probably mutter a monosyllable which is not 'mice.'

Of course, school is merely a preparation for living; unless one goes to a university, in which case it is a preparation for university. One is supposed to turn one's attention to living when these preliminaries are over—say at the age of about twenty. Assuredly one lives then; there is, however, nothing new in that, for one has been living all the time, in a fashion; all the time one has been using the machine without understanding it. But does one, school and college being over, enter upon a study of the machine? Not a bit. The question then becomes, not how to live, but how to obtain and retain a position in which one will be able to live; how to get minute portions of dead animals and plants which one can swallow, in order not to die of hunger; how to acquire and constantly renew a stock of other portions of dead animals and plants in which one can envelop oneself in order not to die of cold; how to procure the exclusive right of entry into certain huts where one may sleep and eat without being rained upon by the clouds of heaven. And so forth. And when one has realised this ambition, there comes the desire to be able to double the operation and do it, not for oneself alone, but for oneself and another. Marriage! But no scientific sustained attention is yet given to the real business of living, of smooth intercourse, of self-expression, of conscious adaptation to environment—in brief, to the study of the machine. At thirty the chances are that a man will understand better the draught of a chimney than his own respiratory apparatus—to name one of the simple, obvious things—and as for understanding the working of his own brain—what an idea! As for the skill to avoid the waste of power involved by friction in the business of living, do we give an hour to it in a month? Do we ever at all examine it save in an amateurish and clumsy fashion? A young lady produces a water-colour drawing. 'Very nice!' we say, and add, to ourselves, 'For an amateur.' But our living is more amateurish than that young lady's drawing; though surely we ought every one of us to be professionals at living!

When we have been engaged in the preliminaries to living for about fifty-five years, we begin to think about slacking off. Up till this period our reason for not having scientifically studied the art of living—the perfecting and use of the finer parts of the machine—is not that we have lacked leisure (most of us have enormous heaps of leisure), but that we have simply been too absorbed in the preliminaries, have, in fact, treated the preliminaries to the business as the business itself. Then at fifty-five we ought at last to begin to live our lives with professional skill, as a professional painter paints pictures. Yes, but we can't. It is too late then. Neither painters, nor acrobats, nor any professionals can be formed at the age of fifty-five. Thus we finish our lives amateurishly, as we have begun them. And when the machine creaks and sets our teeth on edge, or refuses to obey the steering-wheel and deposits us in the ditch, we say: 'Can't be helped!' or 'Doesn't matter! It will be all the same a hundred years hence!' or: 'I must make the best of things.' And we try to believe that in accepting the *status quo* we have justified the *status quo*, and all the time we feel our insincerity.

You exclaim that I exaggerate. I do. To force into prominence an aspect of affairs usually overlooked, it is absolutely necessary to exaggerate. Poetic licence is one name for this kind of exaggeration. But I exaggerate very little indeed, much less than perhaps you think. I know that you are going to point out to me that vast numbers of people regularly spend a considerable portion of their leisure in striving after self-improvement. Granted! And I am glad of it. But I should be gladder if their strivings bore more closely upon the daily business of living, of self-expression without friction and without futile desires. See this man who regularly studies every evening of his life! He has genuinely understood the nature of poetry, and his taste is admirable. He recites verse with true feeling, and may be said to be highly cultivated. Poetry is a continual source of pleasure to him. True! But why is he always complaining about not receiving his deserts in the office? Why is he worried about finance? Why does he so often sulk with his wife? Why does he persist in eating more than his digestion will tolerate? It was not written in the book of fate that he should complain and worry and sulk and suffer. And if he was a professional at living he would not do these things. There is no reason why he should do them, except the reason that he has never learnt his business, never studied the human machine as a whole, never really thought rationally about living. Supposing you encountered an automobilist who was swerving and grinding all over the road, and you stopped to ask what was the matter, and he replied: 'Never mind what's the matter. Just look at my lovely acetylene lamps, how they shine, and how I've polished them!' You would not regard him as a Clifford-Earp, or even as an entirely sane man. So with our student of poetry. It is indubitable that a large amount of what is known as self-improvement is simply self-indulgence—a form of pleasure which only incidentally improves a particular part of the machine, and even that to the neglect of far more important parts.

My aim is to direct a man's attention to himself as a whole, considered as a machine, complex and capable of quite extraordinary efficiency, for travelling through this world smoothly, in any desired manner, with satisfaction not only to himself but to the people he meets *en route*, and the people who are overtaking him and whom he is overtaking. My aim is to show that only an inappreciable fraction of our ordered and sustained efforts is given to the business of actual living, as distinguished from the preliminaries to living.

III

THE BRAIN AS A GENTLEMAN-AT-LARGE

It is not as if, in this business of daily living, we were seriously hampered by ignorance either as to the results which we ought to obtain, or as to the general means which we must employ in order to obtain them. With all our absorption in the mere preliminaries to living, and all our carelessness about living itself, we arrive pretty soon at a fairly accurate notion of what satisfactory living is, and we perceive with some clearness the methods necessary to success. I have pictured the man who wakes up in the middle of the night and sees the horrid semi-fiasco of his life. But let me picture the man who wakes up refreshed early on a fine summer morning and looks into his mind with the eyes of hope and experience, not experience and despair. That man will pass a delightful half-hour in thinking upon the scheme of the universe as it affects himself. He is quite clear that contentment depends on his own acts, and that no power can prevent him from performing those acts. He plans everything out, and before he gets up he knows precisely what he must and will do in certain foreseen crises and junctures. He sincerely desires to live efficiently—who would wish to make a daily mess of existence?—and he knows the way to realise the desire.

And yet, mark me! That man will not have been an hour on his feet on this difficult earth before the machine has unmistakably gone wrong: the machine which was designed to do this work of living, which is capable of doing it thoroughly well, but which has not been put into order! What is the use of consulting the map of life and tracing the itinerary, and getting the machine out of the shed, and making a start, if half the nuts are loose, or the steering pillar is twisted, or there is no petrol in the tank? (Having asked this question, I will drop the mechanico-vehicular comparison, which is too rough and crude for the delicacy of the subject.) Where has the human machine gone wrong? It has gone wrong in the brain. What, is he 'wrong in the head'? Most assuredly, most strictly. He knows—none better—that when his wife employs a particular tone containing ten grains of asperity, and he replies in a particular tone containing eleven grains, the consequences will be explosive. He knows, on the other hand, that if he replies in a tone containing only one little drop of honey, the consequences may not be unworthy of two reasonable beings. He knows this. His brain is fully instructed. And lo! his brain, while arguing that women are really too absurd (as if that was the point), is sending down orders to the muscles of the throat and mouth which result in at least eleven grains of asperity, and conjugal relations are endangered for the day. He didn't want to do it. His desire was not to do it. He despises himself for doing it. But his brain was not in working order. His brain ran away—'raced'—on its own account, against reason, against desire, against morning resolves—and there he is!

That is just one example, of the simplest and slightest. Examples can be multiplied. The man may be a young man whose immediate future depends on his passing an examination—an examination which he is capable of passing 'on his head,' which nothing can prevent him from passing if only his brain will not be so absurd as to give orders to his legs to walk out of the house towards the tennis court instead of sending them upstairs to the study; if only, having once safely lodged him in the study, his brain will devote itself to the pages of books instead of dwelling on the image of a nice girl—not at all like other girls. Or the man may be an old man who will live in perfect comfort if only his brain will not interminably run round and round in a circle of grievances, apprehensions, and fears which no amount of contemplation can destroy or even ameliorate.

The brain, the brain—that is the seat of trouble! 'Well,' you say, 'of course it is. We all know that!' We don't act as if we did, anyway. 'Give us more brains, Lord!' ejaculated a great writer. Personally, I think he would have been wiser if he had asked first for the power to keep in order such brains as we have. We indubitably possess quite enough brains, quite as much as we can handle. The supreme muddlers of living are often people of quite remarkable intellectual faculty, with a quite remarkable gift of being wise for others. The pity is that our brains have a way of 'wandering,' as it is politely called. Brain-wandering is indeed now recognised as a specific disease. I wonder what you, O business man with an office in Ludgate Circus, would say to your office-boy, whom you had dispatched on an urgent message to Westminster, and whom you found larking around Euston Station when you rushed to catch your week-end train. 'Please, sir, I started to go to Westminster, but there's something funny in my limbs that makes me go up all manner of streets. I can't help it, sir!' 'Can't you?' you would say. 'Well, you had better go and be somebody else's office-boy.' Your brain is something worse than that office-boy, something more insidiously potent for evil.

I conceive the brain of the average well-intentioned man as possessing the tricks and manners of one of those gentlemen-at-large who, having nothing very urgent to do, stroll along and offer their services gratis to some shorthanded work of philanthropy. They will commonly demoralise and disorganise the business conduct of an affair in about a fortnight. They come when they like; they go when they like. Sometimes they are exceedingly industrious and obedient, but then there is an even chance that they will shirk and follow their own sweet will. And they mustn't be spoken to, or pulled up—for have they not kindly volunteered, and are they not giving their days for naught! These persons are the bane of the enterprises in which they condescend to meddle. Now, there is a vast deal too much of the gentleman-at-large about one's brain. One's brain has no right whatever to behave as a gentleman-at-large: but it in fact does. It forgets; it flatly ignores orders; at the critical moment when pressure is highest, it simply lights a cigarette and goes out for a walk. And we meekly sit down under this behaviour! 'I didn't feel like stewing,' says the young man who, against his wish, will fail in his examination. 'The words were out of my mouth before I knew it,' says the husband whose wife is a woman. 'I couldn't get any inspiration to-day,' says the artist. 'I can't resist Stilton,' says the fellow who is dying of greed. 'One can't help one's thoughts,' says the old worrier. And this last really voices the secret excuse of all five.

And you all say to me: 'My brain is myself. How can I alter myself? I was born like that.' In the first place you were not born 'like that,' you have lapsed to that. And in the second place your brain is not yourself. It is only a part of yourself, and not the highest seat of authority. Do you love your mother, wife, or children with your brain? Do you desire with your brain? Do you, in a word, ultimately and essentially *live* with your brain? No. Your brain is an instrument. The proof that it is an instrument lies in the fact that, when extreme necessity urges, *you* can command your brain to do certain things, and it does them. The first of the two great principles which underlie the efficiency of the human machine is this: *The brain is a servant, exterior to the central force of the Ego*. If it is out of control the reason is not that it is uncontrollable, but merely that its discipline has been neglected. The brain can be trained, as the hand and eye can be trained; it can be made as obedient as a sporting dog, and by similar methods. In the meantime the indispensable preparation for brain discipline is to form the habit of regarding one's brain as an instrument exterior to one's self, like a tongue or a foot.

IV

THE FIRST PRACTICAL STEP

The brain is a highly quaint organism. Let me say at once, lest I should be cannonaded by physiologists, psychologists, or metaphysicians, that by the 'brain' I mean the faculty which reasons and which gives orders to the muscles. I mean exactly what the plain man means by the brain. The brain is the diplomatist which arranges relations between our instinctive self and the universe, and it fulfils its mission when it provides for the maximum of freedom to the instincts with the minimum of friction. It argues with the instincts. It takes them on one side and points out the unwisdom of certain performances. It catches them by the coat-tails when they are about to make fools of themselves. 'Don't drink all that iced champagne at a draught,' it says to one instinct; 'we may die of it.' 'Don't catch that rude fellow one in the eye,' it says to another instinct; 'he is more powerful than us.' It is, in fact, a majestic spectacle of common sense. And yet it has the most extraordinary lapses. It is just like that man—we all know him and consult him—who is a continual fount of excellent, sagacious advice on everything, but who somehow cannot bring his sagacity to bear on his own personal career.

In the matter of its own special activities the brain is usually undisciplined and unreliable. We never know what it will do next. We give it some work to do, say, as we are walking along the street to the office. Perhaps it has to devise some scheme for making £150 suffice for £200, or perhaps it has to plan out the heads of a very important letter. We meet a pretty woman, and away that undisciplined, sagacious brain runs after her, dropping the scheme or the draft letter, and amusing itself with aspirations or regrets for half an hour, an hour, sometimes a day. The serious part of our instinctive self feebly remonstrates, but without effect. Or it may be that we have suffered a great disappointment, which is definite and hopeless. Will the brain, like a sensible creature, leave that disappointment alone, and instead of living in the past live in the present or the future? Not it! Though it knows perfectly well that it is wasting its time and casting a very painful and utterly unnecessary gloom over itself and us, it can so little control its unhealthy morbid appetite that no expostulations will induce it to behave rationally. Or perhaps, after a confabulation with the soul, it has been decided that when next a certain harmful instinct comes into play the brain shall firmly interfere. 'Yes,' says the brain, 'I really will watch that.' But when the moment arrives, is the brain on the spot? The brain has probably forgotten the affair entirely, or remembered it too late; or sighs, as the victorious instinct knocks it on the head: 'Well, *next* time!'

All this, and much more that every reader can supply from his own exciting souvenirs, is absurd and ridiculous on the part of the brain. It is a conclusive proof that the brain is out of condition, idle as a nigger, capricious as an actor-manager, and eaten to the core with loose habits. Therefore the brain must be put into training. It is the most important part of the human machine by which the soul expresses and develops itself, and it must learn good habits. And primarily it must be taught obedience. Obedience can only be taught by imposing one's will, by the sheer force of volition. And the brain must be mastered by will-power. The beginning of wise living lies in the control of the brain by the will; so that the brain may act according to the precepts which the brain itself gives. With an obedient disciplined brain a man may live always right up to the standard of his best moments.

To teach a child obedience you tell it to do something, and you see that that something is done. The same with the brain. Here is the foundation of an efficient life and the antidote for the tendency to make a fool of oneself. It is marvellously simple. Say to your brain: 'From 9 o'clock to 9.30 this morning you must dwell without ceasing on a particular topic which I will give you.' Now, it doesn't matter what this topic is—the point is to control and invigorate the brain by exercise—but you may just as well give it a useful topic to think over as a futile one. You might give it this: 'My brain is my servant. I am not the play-thing of my brain.' Let it concentrate on these statements for thirty minutes. 'What?' you cry. 'Is this the way to an efficient life? Why, there's nothing in it!' Simple as it may appear, this *is* the way, and it is the only way. As for there being nothing in it, try it. I guarantee that you will fail to keep your brain concentrated on the given idea for thirty seconds—let alone thirty minutes. You will find your brain conducting itself in a manner which would be comic were it not tragic. Your first experiments will result in disheartening failure, for to exact from the brain, at will and by will, concentration on a given idea for even so short a period as half an hour is an exceedingly difficult feat—and a fatiguing! It needs perseverance. It needs a terrible obstinacy on the part of the will. That brain of yours will be hopping about all over the place, and every time it hops you must bring it back by force to its original position. You must absolutely compel it to ignore every idea except the one which you have selected for its attention. You cannot hope to triumph all at once. But you can hope to triumph. There is no royal road to the control of the brain. There is no patent dodge about it, and no complicated function which a plain person may not comprehend. It is simply a question of: 'I will, *I* will, and I *will*.' (Italics here are indispensable.)

Let me resume. Efficient living, living up to one's best standard, getting the last ounce of power out of the machine with the minimum of friction: these things depend on the disciplined and vigorous condition of the brain. The brain can be disciplined by learning the habit of obedience. And it can learn the habit of obedience by the practice of concentration. Disciplinary concentration, though nothing could have the air of being simpler, is the basis of the whole structure. This fact must be grasped imaginatively; it must be seen and felt. The more regularly concentration is practised, the more firmly will the imagination grasp the effects of it, both direct and indirect. After but a few days of honest trying in the exercise which I have indicated, you will perceive its influence. You will grow accustomed to the idea, at first strange in its novelty, of the brain being external to the supreme force which is *you*, and in subjection to that force. You will, as a not very distant possibility, see yourself in possession of the power to switch your brain on and off in a particular subject as you switch electricity on and off in a particular room. The brain will get used to the straight paths of obedience. And—a remarkable phenomenon—it will, by the mere practice of obedience, become less forgetful and more effective. It will not so frequently give way to an instinct that takes it by surprise. In a word, it will have received a general tonic. With a brain that is improving every day you can set about the perfecting of the machine in a scientific manner.

V

HABIT-FORMING BY CONCENTRATION

As soon as the will has got the upper hand of the brain—as soon as it can say to the brain, with a fair certainty of being obeyed: 'Do this. Think along these lines, and continue to do so without wandering until I give you leave to stop'—then is the time arrived when the perfecting of the human machine may be undertaken in a large and comprehensive spirit, as a city council undertakes the purification and reconstruction of a city. The tremendous possibilities of an obedient brain will be perceived immediately we begin to reflect upon what we mean by our 'character.' Now, a person's character is, and can be, nothing else but the total result of his habits of thought. A person is benevolent because he habitually thinks benevolently. A person is idle because his thoughts dwell habitually on the instant pleasures of idleness. It is true that everybody is born with certain predispositions, and that these predispositions influence very strongly the early formation of habits of thought. But the fact remains that the character is built by long-continued habits of thought. If the mature edifice of character usually shows in an exaggerated form the peculiarities of the original predisposition, this merely indicates a probability that the slow erection of the edifice has proceeded at haphazard, and that reason has not presided over it. A child may be born with a tendency to bent shoulders. If nothing is done, if on the contrary he becomes a clerk and abhors gymnastics, his shoulders will develop an excessive roundness, entirely through habit. Whereas, if his will, guided by his reason, had compelled the formation of a corrective physical habit, his shoulders might have been, if not quite straight, nearly so. Thus a physical habit! The same with a mental habit.

The more closely we examine the development of original predispositions, the more clearly we shall see that this development is not inevitable, is not a process which works itself out independently according to mysterious, ruthless laws which we cannot understand. For instance, the effect of an original predisposition may be destroyed by an accidental shock. A young man with an inherited tendency to alcohol may develop into a stern teetotaller through the shock caused by seeing his drunken father strike his mother; whereas, if his father had chanced to be affectionate in drink, the son might have ended in the gutter. No ruthless law here! It is notorious, also, that natures are sometimes completely changed in their development by chance momentary contact with natures stronger than themselves. 'From that day I resolved—' etc. You know the phrase. Often the resolve is not kept; but often it is kept. A spark has inflamed the will. The burning will has tyrannised over the brain. New habits have been formed. And the result looks just like a miracle.

Now, if these great transformations can be brought about by accident, cannot similar transformations be brought about by a reasonable design? At any rate, if one starts to bring them about, one starts with the assurance that transformations are not impossible, since they have occurred. One starts also in the full knowledge of the influence of habit on life. Take any one of your own habits, mental or physical. You will be able to recall the time when that habit did not exist, or if it did exist it was scarcely perceptible. And you will discover that nearly all your habits have been formed unconsciously, by daily repetitions which bore no relation to a general plan, and which you practised not noticing. You will be compelled to admit that your 'character,' as it is to-day, is a structure that has been built almost without the aid of an architect; higgledy-piggledy, anyhow. But occasionally the architect did step in and design something. Here and there among your habits you will find one that you consciously and of deliberate purpose initiated and persevered with—doubtless owing to some happy influence. What is the difference between that conscious habit and the unconscious habits? None whatever as regards its effect on the sum of your character. It may be the strongest of all your habits. The only quality that differentiates it from the others is that it has a definite object (most likely a good object), and that it wholly or partially fulfils that object. There is not a man who reads these lines but has, in this detail or that, proved in himself that the will, forcing the brain to repeat the same action again and again, can modify the shape of his character as a sculptor modifies the shape of damp clay.

But if a grown man's character is developing from day to day (as it is), if nine-tenths of the development is due to unconscious action and one-tenth to conscious action, and if the one-tenth conscious is the most satisfactory part of the total result; why, in the name of common sense, henceforward, should not nine-tenths, instead of one-tenth, be due to conscious action? What is there to prevent this agreeable consummation? There is nothing whatever to prevent it—except insubordination on the part of the brain. And insubordination of the brain can be cured, as I have previously shown. When I see men unhappy and inefficient in the craft of *living*, from sheer, crass inattention to their own development; when I see misshapen men building up businesses and empires, and never stopping to build up themselves; when I see dreary men expending precisely the same energy on teaching a dog to walk on its hind-legs as would brighten the whole colour of their own lives, I feel as if I wanted to give up the ghost, so ridiculous, so fatuous does the spectacle seem! But, of course, I do not give up the ghost. The paroxysm passes. Only I really must cry out: 'Can't you see what you're missing? Can't you see that you're missing the most interesting thing on earth, far more interesting than businesses, empires, and dogs? Doesn't it strike you how clumsy and short-sighted you are—working always with an inferior machine when you might have a smooth-gliding perfection? Doesn't it strike you how badly you are treating yourself?'

Listen, you confirmed grumbler, you who make the evening meal hideous with complaints against destiny—for it is you I will single out. Are you aware what people are saying about you behind your back? They are saying that you render yourself and your family miserable by the habit which has grown on you of always grumbling. 'Surely it isn't as bad as that?' you protest. Yes, it is just as bad as that. You say: 'The fact is, I know it's absurd to grumble. But I'm like that. I've tried to stop it, and I can't!' How have you tried to stop it? 'Well, I've made up my mind several times to fight against it, but I never succeed. This is strictly between ourselves. I don't usually admit that I'm a grumbler.' Considering that you grumble for about an hour and a half every day of your life, it was sanguine, my dear sir, to expect to cure such a habit by means of a solitary intention, formed at intervals in the brain and then forgotten. No! You must do more than that. If you will daily fix your brain firmly for half an hour on the truth (you know it to be a truth) that grumbling is absurd and futile, your brain will henceforward begin to form a habit in that direction; it will begin to be moulded to the idea that grumbling is absurd and futile. In odd moments, when it isn't thinking of anything in particular, it will suddenly remember that grumbling is absurd and futile. When you sit down to the meal and open your mouth to say: 'I can't think what my ass of a partner means by—' it will remember that grumbling is absurd and futile, and will alter the arrangement of your throat, teeth, and tongue, so that you will say: 'What fine weather we're having!' In brief, it will remember involuntarily, by a new habit. All who look into their experience will admit that the failure to replace old habits by new ones is due to the fact that at the critical moment the brain does not remember; it simply forgets. The practice of concentration will cure that. All depends on regular concentration. This grumbling is an instance, though chosen not quite at hazard.

VI

LORD OVER THE NODDLE

Having proved by personal experiment the truth of the first of the two great principles which concern the human machine—namely, that the brain is a servant, not a master, and can be controlled—we may now come to the second. The second is more fundamental than the first, but it can be of no use until the first is understood and put into practice. The human machine is an apparatus of brain and muscle for enabling the Ego to develop freely in the universe by which it is surrounded, without friction. Its function is to convert the facts of the universe to the best advantage of the Ego. The facts of the universe are the material with which it is its business to deal—not the facts of an ideal universe, but the facts of this universe. Hence, when friction occurs, when the facts of the universe cease to be of advantage to the Ego, the fault is in the machine. It is not the solar system that has gone wrong, but the human machine. Second great principle, therefore:

'*In case of friction, the machine is always at fault.*'

You can control nothing but your own mind. Even your two-year-old babe may defy you by the instinctive force of its personality. But your own mind you can control. Your own mind is a sacred enclosure into which nothing harmful can enter except by your permission. Your own mind has the power to transmute every external phenomenon to its own purposes. If happiness arises from cheerfulness, kindliness, and rectitude (and who will deny it?), what possible combination of circumstances is going to make you unhappy so long as the machine remains in order? If self-development consists in the utilisation of one's environment (not utilisation of somebody else's environment), how can your environment prevent you from developing? You would look rather foolish without it, anyway. In that noddle of yours is everything necessary for development, for the maintaining of dignity, for the achieving of happiness, and you are absolute lord over the noddle, will you but exercise the powers of lordship. Why worry about the contents of somebody else's noddle, in which you can be nothing but an intruder, when you may arrive at a better result, with absolute certainty, by confining your activities to your own? 'Look within.' 'The Kingdom of Heaven is within you.' 'Oh, yes!' you protest. 'All that's old. Epictetus said that. Marcus Aurelius said that. Christ said that.' They did. I admit it readily. But if you were ruffled this morning because your motor-omnibus broke down, and you had to take a cab, then so far as you are concerned these great teachers lived in vain. You, calling yourself a reasonable man, are going about dependent for your happiness, dignity, and growth, upon a thousand things over which you have no control, and the most exquisitely organised machine for ensuring happiness, dignity, and growth, is rusting away inside you. And all because you have a sort of notion that a saying said two thousand years ago cannot be practical.

You remark sagely to your child: 'No, my child, you cannot have that moon, and you will accomplish nothing by crying for it. Now, here is this beautiful box of bricks, by means of which you may amuse yourself while learning many wonderful matters and improving your mind. You must try to be content with what you have, and to make the best of it. If you had the moon you wouldn't be any happier.' Then you lie awake half the night repining because the last post has brought a letter to the effect that 'the Board cannot entertain your application for,' etc. You say the two cases are not alike. They are not. Your child has never heard of Epictetus. On the other hand, justice *is* the moon. At your age you surely know that. 'But the Directors *ought* to have granted my application,' you insist. Exactly! I agree. But we are not in a universe of *oughts*. You have a special apparatus within you for dealing with a universe where *oughts* are flagrantly disregarded. And you are not using it. You are lying awake, keeping your wife awake, injuring your health, injuring hers, losing your dignity and your cheerfulness. Why? Because you think that these antics and performances will influence the Board? Because you think that they will put you into a better condition for dealing with your environment to-morrow? Not a bit. Simply because the machine is at fault.

In certain cases we do make use of our machines (as well as their sad condition of neglect will allow), but in other cases we behave in an extraordinarily irrational manner. Thus if we sally out and get caught in a heavy shower we do not, unless very far gone in foolishness, sit down and curse the weather. We put up our umbrella, if we have one, and if not we hurry home. We may grumble, but it is not serious grumbling; we accept the shower as a fact of the universe, and control ourselves. Thus also, if by a sudden catastrophe we lose somebody who is important to us, we grieve, but we control ourselves, recognising one of those hazards of destiny from which not even millionaires are exempt. And the result on our Ego is usually to improve it in essential respects. But there are other strokes of destiny, other facts of the universe, against which we protest as a child protests when deprived of the moon.

Take the case of an individual with an imperfect idea of honesty. Now, that individual is the consequence of his father and mother and his environment, and his father and mother of theirs, and so backwards to the single-celled protoplasm. That individual is a result of the cosmic order, the inevitable product of cause and effect. We know that. We must admit that he is just as much a fact of the universe as a shower of rain or a storm at sea that swallows a ship. We freely grant in the abstract that there must be, at the present stage of evolution, a certain number of persons with unfair minds. We are quite ready to contemplate such an individual with philosophy—until it happens that, in the course of the progress of the solar system, he runs up against ourselves. Then listen to the outcry! Listen to the continual explosions of a righteous man aggrieved! The individual may be our clerk, cashier, son, father, brother, partner, wife, employer. We are ill-used! We are being treated unfairly! We kick; we scream. We nourish the inward sense of grievance that eats the core out of content. We sit down in the rain. We decline to think of umbrellas, or to run to shelter.

We care not that that individual is a fact which the universe has been slowly manufacturing for millions of years. Our attitude implies that we want eternity to roll back and begin again, in such wise that we at any rate shall not be disturbed. Though we have a machine for the transmutation of facts into food for our growth, we do not dream of using it. But, we say, he is doing us harm! Where? In our minds. He has robbed us of our peace, our comfort, our happiness, our good temper. Even if he has, we might just as well inveigh against a shower. But has he? What was our brain doing while this naughty person stepped in and robbed us of the only possessions worth having? No, no! It is not that he has done us harm—the one cheerful item in a universe of stony facts is that no one can harm anybody except himself—it is merely that we have been silly, precisely as silly as if we had taken a seat in the rain with a folded umbrella by our side.... The machine is at fault. I fancy we are now obtaining glimpses of what that phrase really means.

VII
WHAT 'LIVING' CHIEFLY IS

It is in intercourse—social, sentimental, or business—with one's fellows that the qualities and the condition of the human machine are put to the test and strained. That part of my life which I conduct by myself, without reference—or at any rate without direct reference—to others, I can usually manage in such a way that the gods do not positively weep at the spectacle thereof. My environment is simpler, less puzzling, when I am alone, my calm and my self-control less liable to violent fluctuations. Impossible to be disturbed by a chair! Impossible that a chair should get on one's nerves! Impossible to blame a chair for not being as reasonable, as archangelic as I am myself! But when it comes to people!... Well, that is 'living,' then! The art of life, the art of extracting all its power from the human machine, does not lie chiefly in processes of bookish-culture, nor in contemplations of the beauty and majesty of existence. It lies chiefly in keeping the peace, the whole peace, and nothing but the peace, with those with whom one is 'thrown.' Is it in sitting ecstatic over Shelley, Shakespeare, or Herbert Spencer, solitary in my room of a night, that I am 'improving myself' and learning to live? Or is it in watching over all my daily human contacts? Do not seek to escape the comparison by insinuating that I despise study, or by pointing out that the eternal verities are beyond dailiness. Nothing of the kind! I am so 'silly' about books that merely to possess them gives me pleasure. And if the verities are good for eternity they ought to be good for a day. If I cannot exchange them for daily coin—if I can't buy happiness for a single day because I've nothing less than an eternal verity about me and nobody has sufficient change—then my eternal verity is not an eternal verity. It is merely an unnegotiable bit of glass (called a diamond), or even a note on the Bank of Engraving.

I can say to myself when I arise in the morning: 'I am master of my brain. No one can get in there and rage about like a bull in a china shop. If my companions on the planet's crust choose to rage about they cannot affect *me*! I will not let them. I have power to maintain my own calm, and I will. No earthly being can force me to be false to my principles, or to be blind to the beauty of the universe, or to be gloomy, or to be irritable, or to complain against my lot. For these things depend on the brain; cheerfulness, kindliness, and honest thinking are all within the department of the brain. The disciplined brain can accomplish them. And my brain is disciplined, and I will discipline it more and more as the days pass. I am, therefore, independent of hazard, and I will back myself to conduct all intercourse as becomes a rational creature.' ... I can say this. I can ram this argument by force of will into my brain, and by dint of repeating it often enough I shall assuredly arrive at the supreme virtues of reason. I should assuredly conquer—the brain being such a machine of habit—even if I did not take the trouble to consider in the slightest degree what manner of things my fellow-men are—by acting merely in my own interests. But the way of perfection (I speak relatively) will be immensely shortened and smoothed if I do consider, dispassionately, the case of the other human machines. Thus:—

The truth is that my attitude towards my fellows is fundamentally and totally wrong, and that it entails on my thinking machine a strain which is quite unnecessary, though I may have arranged the machine so as to withstand the strain successfully. The secret of smooth living is a calm cheerfulness which will leave me always in full possession of my reasoning faculty—in order that I may live by reason instead of by instinct and momentary passion. The secret of calm cheerfulness is kindliness; no person can be consistently cheerful and calm who does not consistently think kind thoughts. But how can I be kindly when I pass the major portion of my time in blaming the people who surround me—who are part of my environment? If I, blaming, achieve some approach to kindliness, it is only by a great and exhausting effort of self-mastery. The inmost secret, then, lies in not blaming, in not judging and emitting verdicts. Oh! I do not blame by word of mouth! I am far too advanced for such a puerility. I keep the blame in my own breast, where it festers. I am always privately forgiving, which is bad for me. Because, you know, there is nothing to forgive. I do not have to forgive bad weather; nor, if I found myself in an earthquake, should I have to forgive the earthquake.

All blame, uttered or unexpressed, is wrong. I do not blame myself. I can explain myself to myself. I can invariably explain myself. If I forged a friend's name on a cheque I should explain the affair quite satisfactorily to myself. And instead of blaming myself I should sympathise with myself for having been driven into such an excessively awkward corner. Let me examine honestly my mental processes, and I must admit that my attitude towards others is entirely different from my attitude towards myself. I must admit that in the seclusion of my mind, though I say not a word, I am constantly blaming others because I am not happy. Whenever I bump up against an opposing personality and my smooth progress is impeded, I secretly blame the opposer. I act as though I had shouted to the world: 'Clear out of the way, every one, for I am coming!' Every one does not clear out of the way. I did not really expect every one to clear out of the way. But I act, within, as though I had so expected. I blame. Hence kindliness, hence cheerfulness, is rendered vastly more difficult for me.

What I ought to do is this! I ought to reflect again and again, and yet again, that the beings among whom I have to steer, the living environment out of which I have to manufacture my happiness, are just as inevitable in the scheme of evolution as I am myself; have just as much right to be themselves as I have to be myself; are precisely my equals in the face of Nature; are capable of being explained as I am capable of being explained; are entitled to the same latitude as I am entitled to, and are no more responsible for their composition and their environment than I for mine. I ought to reflect again and again, and yet again, that they all deserve from me as much sympathy as I give to myself. Why not? Having thus reflected in a general manner, I ought to take one by one the individuals with whom I am brought into frequent contact, and seek, by a deliberate effort of the imagination and the reason, to understand them, to understand why they act thus and thus, what their difficulties are, what their 'explanation' is, and how friction can be avoided. So I ought to reflect, morning after morning, until my brain is saturated with the cases of these individuals. Here is a course of discipline. If I follow it I shall gradually lose the preposterous habit of blaming, and I shall have laid the foundations of that quiet, unshakable self-possession which is the indispensable preliminary of conduct according to reason, of thorough efficiency in the machine of happiness. But something in me, something distinctly base, says: 'Yes. The put-yourself-in-his-place business over again! The do-unto-others business over again!' Just so! Something in me is ashamed of being 'moral.' (You all know the feeling!) Well, morals are naught but another name for reasonable conduct; a higher and more practical form of egotism—an egotism which, while freeing others, frees myself. I have tried the lower form of egotism. And it has failed. If I am afraid of being moral, if I prefer to cut off my nose to spite my face, well, I must accept the consequences. But truth will prevail.

VIII
THE DAILY FRICTION

It is with common daily affairs that I am now dealing, not with heroic enterprises, ambitions, martyrdoms. Take the day, the ordinary day in the ordinary house or office. Though it comes seven times a week, and is the most banal thing imaginable, it is quite worth attention. How does the machine get through it? Ah! the best that can be said of the machine is that it does get through it, somehow. The friction, though seldom such as to bring matters to a standstill, is frequent—the sort of friction that, when it occurs in a bicycle, is just sufficient to annoy the rider, but not sufficient to make him get off the machine and examine the bearings. Occasionally the friction is very loud; indeed, disturbing, and at rarer intervals it shrieks, like an omnibus brake out of order. You know those days when you have the sensation that life is not large enough to contain the household or the office-staff, when the business of intercourse may be compared to the manoeuvres of two people who, having awakened with a bad headache, are obliged to dress simultaneously in a very small bedroom. 'After you with that towel!' in accents of bitter, grinding politeness. 'If you could kindly move your things off this chair!' in a voice that would blow brains out if it were a bullet. I venture to say that you know those days. 'But,' you reply, 'such days are few. Usually...!' Well, usually, the friction, though less intense, is still proceeding. We grow accustomed to it. We scarcely notice it, as a person in a stuffy chamber will scarcely notice the stuffiness. But the deteriorating influence due to friction goes on, even if unperceived. And one morning we perceive its ravages—and write a letter to the *Telegraph* to inquire whether life is worth living, or whether marriage is a failure, or whether men are more polite than women. The proof that friction, in various and varying degrees, is practically conscious in most households lies in the fact that when we chance on a household where there is no friction we are startled. We can't recover from the phenomenon. And in describing this household to our friends, we say: 'They get on so well together,' as if we were saying: 'They have wings and can fly! Just fancy! Did you ever hear of such a thing?'

Ninety per cent. of all daily friction is caused by tone—mere tone of voice. Try this experiment. Say: 'Oh, you little darling, you sweet pet, you entirely charming creature!' to a baby or a dog; but roar these delightful epithets in the tone of saying: 'You infernal little nuisance! If I hear another sound I'll break every bone in your body!' The baby will infallibly whimper, and the dog will infallibly mouch off. True, a dog is not a human being, neither is a baby. They cannot understand. It is precisely because they cannot understand and articulate words that the experiment is valuable; for it separates the effect of the tone from the effect of the word spoken. He who speaks, speaks twice. His words convey his thought, and his tone conveys his mental attitude towards the person spoken to. And certainly the attitude, so far as friction goes, is more important than the thought. Your wife may say to you: 'I shall buy that hat I spoke to you about.' And you may reply, quite sincerely, 'As you please.' But it will depend on your tone whether you convey: 'As you please. I am sympathetically anxious that your innocent caprices should be indulged.' Or whether you convey: 'As you please. Only don't bother me with hats. I am above hats. A great deal too much money is spent in this house on hats. However, I'm helpless!' Or whether you convey: 'As you please, heart of my heart, but if you would like to be a nice girl, go gently. We're rather tight.' I need not elaborate. I am sure of being comprehended.

As tone is the expression of attitude, it is, of course, caused by attitude. The frictional tone is chiefly due to that general attitude of blame which I have already condemned as being absurd and unjustifiable. As, by constant watchful discipline, we gradually lose this silly attitude of blame, so the tone will of itself gradually change. But the two ameliorations can proceed together, and it is a curious thing that an agreeable tone, artificially and deliberately adopted, will influence the mental attitude almost as much as the mental attitude will influence the tone. If you honestly feel resentful against some one, but, having understood the foolishness of fury, intentionally mask your fury under a persuasive tone, your fury will at once begin to abate. You will be led into a rational train of thought; you will see that after all the object of your resentment has a right to exist, and that he is neither a doormat nor a scoundrel, and that anyhow nothing is to be gained, and much is to be lost, by fury. You will see that fury is unworthy of you.

Do you remember the gentleness of the tone which you employed after the healing of your first quarrel with a beloved companion? Do you remember the persuasive tone which you used when you wanted to obtain something from a difficult person on whom your happiness depended? Why should not your tone always combine these qualities? Why should you not carefully school your tone? Is it beneath you to ensure the largest possible amount of your own 'way' by the simplest means? Or is there at the back of your mind that peculiarly English and German idea that politeness, sympathy, and respect for another immortal soul would imply deplorable weakness on your part? You say that your happiness does not depend on every person whom you happen to speak to. Yes, it does. Your happiness is always dependent on just that person. Produce friction, and you suffer. Idle to argue that the person has no business to be upset by your tone! You have caused avoidable friction, simply because your machine for dealing with your environment was suffering from pride, ignorance, or thoughtlessness. You say I am making a mountain out of a mole-hill. No! I am making a mountain out of ten million mole-hills. And that is what life does. It is the little but continuous causes that have great effects. I repeat: Why not deliberately adopt a gentle, persuasive tone—just to see what the results are? Surely you are not ashamed to be wise. You may smile superiorly as you read this. Yet you know very well that more than once you *have* resolved to use a gentle and persuasive tone on all occasions, and that the sole reason why you had that fearful shindy yesterday with your cousin's sister-in-law was that you had long since failed to keep your resolve. But you were of my mind once, and more than once.

What you have to do is to teach the new habit to your brain by daily concentration on it; by forcing your brain to think of nothing else for half an hour of a morning. After a time the brain will begin to remember automatically. For, of course, the explanation of your previous failures is that your brain, undisciplined, merely forgot at the critical moment. The tone was out of your mouth before your brain had waked up. It is necessary to watch, as though you were a sentinel, not only against the wrong tone, but against the other symptoms of the attitude of blame. Such as the frown. It is necessary to regard yourself constantly, and in minute detail. You lie in bed for half an hour and enthusiastically concentrate on this beautiful new scheme of the right tone. You rise, and because you don't achieve a proper elegance of necktie at the first knotting, you frown and swear and clench your teeth! There is a symptom of the wrong attitude towards your environment. You are awake, but your brain isn't. It is in such a symptom that you may judge yourself. And not a trifling symptom either! If you will frown at a necktie, if you will use language to a necktie which no gentleman should use to a necktie, what will you be capable of to a responsible being?... Yes, it is very difficult. But it can be done.

IX

'FIRE!'

In this business of daily living, of ordinary usage of the machine in hourly intercourse, there occurs sometimes a phenomenon which is the cause of a great deal of trouble, and the result of a very ill-tended machine. It is a phenomenon impossible to ignore, and yet, so shameful is it, so degrading, so shocking, so miserable, that I hesitate to mention it. For one class of reader is certain to ridicule me, loftily saying: 'One really doesn't expect to find this sort of thing in print nowadays!' And another class of reader is certain to get angry. Nevertheless, as one of my main objects in the present book is to discuss matters which 'people don't talk about,' I shall discuss this matter. But my diffidence in doing so is such that I must approach it deviously, describing it first by means of a figure.

Imagine that, looking at a man's house, you suddenly perceive it to be on fire. The flame is scarcely perceptible. You could put it out if you had a free hand. But you have not got a free hand. It is his house, not yours. He may or may not know that his house is burning. You are aware, by experience, however, that if you directed his attention to the flame, the effect of your warning would be exceedingly singular, almost incredible. For the effect would be that he would instantly begin to strike matches, pour on petroleum, and fan the flame, violently resenting interference. Therefore you can only stand and watch, hoping that he will notice the flames before they are beyond control, and extinguish them. The probability is, however, that he will notice the flames too late. And powerless to avert disaster, you are condemned, therefore, to watch the damage of valuable property. The flames leap higher and higher, and they do not die down till they have burned themselves out. You avert your gaze from the spectacle, and until you are gone the owner of the house pretends that nothing has occurred. When alone he curses himself for his carelessness.

The foregoing is meant to be a description of what happens when a man passes through the incendiary experience known as 'losing his temper.' (There! the cat of my chapter is out of the bag!) A man who has lost his temper is simply being 'burnt out.' His constitutes one of the most curious and (for everybody) humiliating spectacles that life offers. It is an insurrection, a boiling over, a sweeping storm. Dignity, common sense, justice are shrivelled up and destroyed. Anarchy reigns. The devil has broken his chain. Instinct is stamping on the face of reason. And in that man civilisation has temporarily receded millions of years. Of course, the thing amounts to a nervous disease, and I think it is almost universal. You at once protest that you never lose your temper—haven't lost your temper for ages! But do you not mean that you have not smashed furniture for ages? These fires are of varying intensities. Some of them burn very dully. Yet they burn. One man loses his temper; another is merely 'ruffled.' But the event is the same in kind. When you are 'ruffled,' when you are conscious of a resentful vibration that surprises all your being, when your voice changes, when you notice a change in the demeanour of your companion, who sees that he has 'touched a tender point,' you may not go to the length of smashing furniture, but you have had a fire, and your dignity is damaged. You admit it to yourself afterwards. I am sure you know what I mean. And I am nearly sure that you, with your courageous candour, will admit that from time to time you suffer from these mysterious 'fires.'

'Temper,' one of the plagues of human society, is generally held to be incurable, save by the vague process of exercising self-control—a process which seldom has any beneficial results. It is regarded now as smallpox used to be regarded—as a visitation of Providence, which must be borne. But I do not hold it to be incurable. I am convinced that it is permanently curable. And its eminent importance as a nuisance to mankind at large deserves, I think, that it should receive particular attention. Anyhow, I am strongly against the visitation of Providence theory, as being unscientific, primitive, and conducive to unashamed *laissez-aller*. A man can be master in his own house. If he cannot be master by simple force of will, he can be master by ruse and wile. I would employ cleverness to maintain the throne of reason when it is likely to be upset in the mind by one of these devastating and disgraceful insurrections of brute instinct.

It is useless for a man in the habit of losing or mislaying his temper to argue with himself that such a proceeding is folly, that it serves no end, and does nothing but harm. It is useless for him to argue that in allowing his temper to stray he is probably guilty of cruelty, and certainly guilty of injustice to those persons who are forced to witness the loss. It is useless for him to argue that a man of uncertain temper in a house is like a man who goes about a house with a loaded revolver sticking from his pocket, and that all considerations of fairness and reason have to be subordinated in that house to the fear of the revolver, and that such peace as is maintained in that house is often a shameful and an unjust peace. These arguments will not be strong enough to prevail against one of the most powerful and capricious of all habits. This habit must be met and conquered (and it *can* be!) by an even more powerful quality in the human mind; I mean the universal human horror of looking ridiculous. The man who loses his temper often thinks he is doing something rather fine and majestic. On the contrary, so far is this from being the fact, he is merely making an ass of himself. He is merely parading himself as an undignified fool, as that supremely contemptible figure—a grown-up baby. He may intimidate a feeble companion by his raging, or by the dark sullenness of a more subdued flame, but in the heart of even the weakest companion is a bedrock feeling of contempt for him. The way in which a man of uncertain temper is treated by his friends proves that they despise him, for they do not treat him as a reasonable being. How should they treat him as a reasonable being when the tenure of his reason is so insecure? And if only he could hear what is said of him behind his back!...

The invalid can cure himself by teaching his brain the habit of dwelling upon his extreme fatuity. Let him concentrate regularly, with intense fixation, upon the ideas: 'When I lose my temper, when I get ruffled, when that mysterious vibration runs through me, I am making a donkey of myself, a donkey, and a donkey! You understand, a preposterous donkey! I am behaving like a great baby. I look a fool. I am a spectacle bereft of dignity. Everybody despises me, smiles at me in secret, disdains the idiotic ass with whom it is impossible to reason.'

Ordinarily the invalid disguises from himself this aspect of his disease, and his brain will instinctively avoid it as much as it can. But in hours of calm he can slowly and regularly force his brain, by the practice of concentration, to familiarise itself with just this aspect, so that in time its instinct will be to think first, and not last, of just this aspect. When he has arrived at that point he is saved. No man who, at the very inception of the fire, is visited with a clear vision of himself as an arrant ass and pitiable object of contempt, will lack the volition to put the fire out. But, be it noted, he will not succeed until he can do it at once. A fire is a fire, and the engines must gallop by themselves out of the station instantly. This means the acquirement of a mental habit. During the preliminary stages of the cure he should, of course, avoid inflammable situations. This is a perfectly simple thing to do, if the brain has been disciplined out of its natural forgetfulness.

X

MISCHIEVOUSLY OVERWORKING IT

I have dealt with the two general major causes of friction in the daily use of the machine. I will now deal with a minor cause, and make an end of mere dailiness. This minor cause—and after all I do not know that its results are so trifling as to justify the epithet 'minor'—is the straining of the machine by forcing it to do work which it was never intended to do. Although we are incapable of persuading our machines to do effectively that which they are bound to do somehow, we continually overburden them with entirely unnecessary and inept tasks. We cannot, it would seem, let things alone.

For example, in the ordinary household the amount of machine horse-power expended in fighting for the truth is really quite absurd. This pure zeal for the establishment and general admission of the truth is usually termed 'contradictoriness.' But, of course, it is not that; it is something higher. My wife states that the Joneses have gone into a new flat, of which the rent is £165 a year. Now, Jones has told me personally that the rent of his new flat is £156 a year. I correct my wife. Knowing that she is in the right, she corrects me. She cannot bear that a falsehood should prevail. It is not a question of £9, it is a question of truth. Her enthusiasm for truth excites my enthusiasm for truth. Five minutes ago I didn't care twopence whether the rent of the Joneses' new flat was £165 or £156 or £1056 a year. But now I care intensely that it is £156. I have formed myself into a select society for the propagating of the truth about the rent of the Joneses' new flat, and my wife has done the same. In eloquence, in argumentative skill, in strict supervision of our tempers, we each of us squander enormous quantities of that h.-p. which is so precious to us. And the net effect is naught.

Now, if one of us two had understood the elementary principles of human engineering, that one would have said (privately): 'Truth is indestructible. Truth will out. Truth is never in a hurry. If it doesn't come out to-day it will come out to-morrow or next year. It can take care of itself. Ultimately my wife (or my husband) will learn the essential cosmic truth about the rent of the Joneses' new flat. I already know it, and the moment when she (or he) knows it also will be the moment of my triumph. She (or he) will not celebrate my triumph openly, but it will be none the less real. And my reputation for accuracy and calm restraint will be consolidated. If, by a rare mischance, I am in error, it will be vastly better for me in the day of my undoing that I have not been too positive now. Besides, nobody has appointed me sole custodian of the great truth concerning the rent of the Joneses' new flat. I was not brought into the world to be a safe-deposit, and more urgent matters summon me to effort.' If one of us had meditated thus, much needless friction would have been avoided and power saved; *amour-propre* would not have been exposed to risks; the sacred cause of truth would not in the least have suffered; and the rent of the Joneses' new flat would anyhow have remained exactly what it is.

In addition to straining the machine by our excessive anxiety for the spread of truth, we give a very great deal too much attention to the state of other people's machines. I cannot too strongly, too sarcastically, deprecate this astonishing habit. It will be found to be rife in nearly every household and in nearly every office. We are most of us endeavouring to rearrange the mechanism in other heads than our own. This is always dangerous and generally futile. Considering the difficulty we have in our own brains, where our efforts are sure of being accepted as well-meant, and where we have at any rate a rough notion of the machine's construction, our intrepidity in adventuring among the delicate adjustments of other brains is remarkable. We are cursed by too much of the missionary spirit. We must needs voyage into the China of our brother's brain, and explain there that things are seriously wrong in that heathen land, and make ourselves unpleasant in the hope of getting them put right. We have all our own brain and body on which to wreak our personality, but this is not enough; we must extend our personality further, just as though we were a colonising world-power intoxicated by the idea of the 'white man's burden.'

One of the central secrets of efficient daily living is to leave our daily companions alone a great deal more than we do, and attend to ourselves. If a daily companion is conducting his life upon principles which you know to be false, and with results which you feel to be unpleasant, the safe rule is to keep your mouth shut. Or if, out of your singular conceit, you are compelled to open it, open it with all precautions, and with the formal politeness you would use to a stranger. Intimacy is no excuse for rough manners, though the majority of us seem to think it is. You are not in charge of the universe; you are in charge of yourself. You cannot hope to manage the universe in your spare time, and if you try you will probably make a mess of such part of the universe as you touch, while gravely neglecting yourself. In every family there is generally some one whose meddlesome interest in other machines leads to serious friction in his own. Criticise less, even in the secrecy of your chamber. And do not blame at all. Accept your environment and adapt yourself to it in silence, instead of noisily attempting to adapt your environment to yourself. Here is true wisdom. You have no business trespassing beyond the confines of your own individuality. In so trespassing you are guilty of impertinence. This is obvious. And yet one of the chief activities of home-life consists in prancing about at random on other people's private lawns. What I say applies even to the relation between parents and children. And though my precept is exaggerated, it is purposely exaggerated in order effectively to balance the exaggeration in the opposite direction.

All individualities, other than one's own, are part of one's environment. The evolutionary process is going on all right, and they are a portion of it. Treat them as inevitable. To assert that they are inevitable is not to assert that they are unalterable. Only the alteration of them is not primarily your affair; it is theirs. Your affair is to use them, as they are, without self-righteousness, blame, or complaint, for the smooth furtherance of your own ends. There is no intention here to rob them of responsibility by depriving them of free-will while saddling *you* with responsibility as a free agent. As your environment they must be accepted as inevitable, because they *are* inevitable. But as centres themselves they have their own responsibility: which is not yours. The historic question: 'Have we free-will, or are we the puppets of determinism?' enters now. As a question it is fascinating and futile. It has never been, and it never will be, settled. The theory of determinism cannot be demolished by argument. But in his heart every man, including the most obstinate supporter of the theory, demolishes it every hour of every day. On the other hand, the theory of free-will can be demolished by ratiocination! So much the worse for ratiocination! *If we regard ourselves as free agents, and the personalities surrounding us as the puppets of determinism*, we shall have arrived at the working compromise from which the finest results of living can be obtained. The philosophic experience of centuries, if it has proved anything, has proved this. And the man who acts upon it in the common, banal contracts and collisions of the difficult experiment which we call daily life, will speedily become convinced of its practical worth.

XI
AN INTERLUDE

For ten chapters you have stood it, but not without protest. I know the feeling which is in your minds, and which has manifested itself in numerous criticisms of my ideas. That feeling may be briefly translated, perhaps, thus: 'This is all very well, but it isn't true, not a bit! It's only a fairy-tale that you have been telling us. Miracles don't happen,' etc. I, on my part, have a feeling that unless I take your feeling in hand at once, and firmly deal with it, I had better put my shutters up, for you will have got into the way of regarding me simply as a source of idle amusement. Already I can perceive, from the expressions of some critics, that, so far as they are concerned, I might just as well not have written a word. Therefore at this point I pause, in order to insist once more upon what I began by saying.

The burden of your criticism is: 'Human nature is always the same. I know my faults. But it is useless to tell me about them. I can't alter them. I was born like that.' The fatal weakness of this argument is, first, that it is based on a complete falsity; and second, that it puts you in an untenable position. Human nature *does* change. Nothing can be more unscientific, more hopelessly mediæval, than to imagine that it does not. It changes like everything else. You can't see it change. True! But then you can't see the grass growing—not unless you arise very early.

Is human nature the same now as in the days of Babylonian civilisation, when the social machine was oiled by drenchings of blood? Is it the same now as in the days of Greek civilisation, when there was no such thing as romantic love between the sexes? Is it the same now as it was during the centuries when constant friction had to provide its own cure in the shape of constant war? Is it the same now as it was on 2nd March 1819, when the British Government officially opposed a motion to consider the severity of the criminal laws (which included capital punishment for cutting down a tree, and other sensible dodges against friction), and were defeated by a majority of only nineteen votes? Is it the same now as in the year 1883, when the first S.P.C.C. was formed in England?

If you consider that human nature is still the same you should instantly go out and make a bonfire of the works of Spencer, Darwin, and Wallace, and then return to enjoy the purely jocular side of the present volume. If you admit that it has changed, let me ask you how it has changed, unless by the continual infinitesimal efforts, *upon themselves*, of individual men, like you and me. Did you suppose it was changed by magic, or by Acts of Parliament, or by the action of groups on persons, and not of persons on groups? Let me tell you that human nature has changed since yesterday. Let me tell you that to-day reason has a more powerful voice in the directing of instinct than it had yesterday. Let me tell you that to-day the friction of the machines is less screechy and grinding than it was yesterday.

'You were born like that, and you can't alter yourself, and so it's no use talking.' If you really believe this, why make any effort at all? Why not let the whole business beautifully slide and yield to your instincts? What object can there be in trying to control yourself in any manner whatever if you are unalterable? Assert yourself to be unalterable, and you assert yourself a fatalist. Assert yourself a fatalist, and you free yourself from all moral responsibility—and other people, too. Well, then, act up to your convictions, if convictions they are. If you can't alter yourself, I can't alter myself, and supposing that I come along and bash you on the head and steal your purse, you can't blame me. You can only, on recovering consciousness, affectionately grasp my hand and murmur: 'Don't apologise, my dear fellow; we can't alter ourselves.'

This, you say, is absurd. It is. That is one of my innumerable points. The truth is, you do not really believe that you cannot alter yourself. What is the matter with you is just what is the matter with me—sheer idleness. You hate getting up in the morning, and to excuse your inexcusable indolence you talk big about Fate. Just as 'patriotism is the last refuge of a scoundrel,' so fatalism is the last refuge of a shirker. But you deceive no one, least of all yourself. You have not, rationally, a leg to stand on. At this juncture, because I have made you laugh, you consent to say: 'I do try, all I can. But I can only alter myself a very little. By constitution I am mentally idle. I can't help that, can I?' Well, so long as you are not the only absolutely unchangeable thing in a universe of change, I don't mind. It is something for you to admit that you can alter yourself even a very little. The difference between our philosophies is now only a question of degree.

In the application of any system of perfecting the machine, no two persons will succeed equally. From the disappointed tone of some of your criticisms it might be fancied that I had advertised a system for making archangels out of tailors' dummies. Such was not my hope. I have no belief in miracles. But I know that when a thing is thoroughly well done it often has the air of being a miracle. My sole aim is to insist that every man shall perfect his machine to the best of *his* powers, not to the best of somebody else's powers. I do not indulge in any hope that a man can be better than his best self. I am, however, convinced that every man fails to be his best self a great deal oftener than he need fail—for the reason that his will-power, be it great or small, is not directed according to the principles of common sense.

Common sense will surely lead a man to ask the question: 'Why did my actions yesterday contradict my reason?' The reply to this question will nearly always be: 'Because at the critical moment I forgot.' The supreme explanation of the abortive results of so many efforts at self-alteration, the supreme explanation of our frequent miserable scurrying into a doctrine of fatalism, is simple forgetfulness. It is not force that we lack, but the skill to remember exactly what our reason would have us do or think at the moment itself. How is this skill to be acquired? It can only be acquired, as skill at games is acquired, by practice; by the training of the organ involved to such a point that the organ acts rightly by instinct instead of wrongly by instinct. There are degrees of success in this procedure, but there is no such phenomenon as complete failure.

Habits which increase friction can be replaced by habits which lessen friction. Habits which arrest development can be replaced by habits which encourage development. And as a habit is formed naturally, so it can be formed artificially, by imitation of the unconscious process, by accustoming the brain to the new idea. Let me, as an example, refer again to the minor subject of daily friction, and, within that subject, to the influence of tone. A man employs a frictional tone through habit. The frictional tone is an instinct with him. But if he had a quarter of an hour to reflect before speaking, and if during that quarter of an hour he could always listen to arguments against the frictional tone, his use of the frictional tone would rapidly diminish; his reason would conquer his instinct. As things are, his instinct conquers his reason by a surprise attack, by taking it unawares. Regular daily concentration of the brain, for a certain period, upon the non-frictional tone, and the immense advantages of its use, will gradually set up in the brain a new habit of thinking about the non-frictional tone; until at length the brain, disciplined, turns to the correct act before the old, silly instinct can capture it; and ultimately a new sagacious instinct will supplant the old one.

This is the rationale. It applies to all habits. Any person can test its efficiency in any habit. I care not whether he be of strong or weak will—he can test it. He will soon see the tremendous difference between merely 'making a good resolution'—(he has been doing that all his life without any very brilliant consequences)—and concentrating the brain for a given time exclusively upon a good resolution. Concentration, the efficient mastery of the brain—all is there!

XII
AN INTEREST IN LIFE

After a certain period of mental discipline, of deliberate habit-forming and habit-breaking, such as I have been indicating, a man will begin to acquire at any rate a superficial knowledge, a nodding acquaintance, with that wonderful and mysterious affair, his brain, and he will also begin to perceive how important a factor in daily life is the control of his brain. He will assuredly be surprised at the miracles which lie between his collar and his hat, in that queer box that he calls his head. For the effects that can be accomplished by mere steady, persistent thinking must appear to be miracles to apprentices in the practice of thought. When once a man, having passed an unhappy day because his clumsy, negligent brain forgot to control his instincts at a critical moment, has said to his brain: 'I will force you, by concentrating you on that particular point, to act efficiently the next time similar circumstances arise,' and when he has carried out his intention, and when the awkward circumstances have recurred, and his brain, disciplined, has done its work, and so prevented unhappiness—then that man will regard his brain with a new eye. 'By Jove!' he will say; 'I've stopped one source of unhappiness, anyway. There was a time when I should have made a fool of myself in a little domestic crisis such as to-day's. But I have gone safely through it. I am all right. She is all right. The atmosphere is not dangerous with undischarged electricity! And all because my brain, being in proper condition, watched firmly over my instincts! I must keep this up.' He will peer into that brain more and more. He will see more and more of its possibilities.

He will have a new and a supreme interest in *life*. A garden is a fairly interesting thing. But the cultivation of a garden is as dull as cold mutton compared to the cultivation of a brain; and wet weather won't interfere with digging, planting, and pruning in the box.

In due season the man whose hobby is his brain will gradually settle down into a daily routine, with which routine he will start the day. The idea at the back of the mind of the ordinary man (by the ordinary man I mean the man whose brain is not his hobby) is almost always this: 'There are several things at present hanging over me—worries, unfulfilled ambitions, unrealised desires. As soon as these things are definitely settled, then I shall begin to live and enjoy myself.' That is the ordinary man's usual idea. He has it from his youth to his old age. He is invariably waiting for something to happen before he really begins to live. I am sure that if you are an ordinary man (of course, you aren't, I know) you will admit that this is true of you; you exist in the hope that one day things will be sufficiently smoothed out for you to begin to live. That is just where you differ from the man whose brain is his hobby. His daily routine consists in a meditation in the following vein: 'This day is before me. The circumstances of this day are my environment; they are the material out of which, by means of my brain, I have to live and be happy and to refrain from causing unhappiness in other people. It is the business of my brain to make use of *this* material. My brain is in its box for that sole purpose. Not to-morrow! Not next year! Not when I have made my fortune! Not when my sick child is out of danger! Not when my wife has returned to her senses! Not when my salary is raised! Not when I have passed that examination! Not when my indigestion is better! But *now!* To-day, exactly as to-day is! The facts of to-day, which in my unregeneracy I regarded primarily as anxieties, nuisances, impediments, I now regard as so much raw material from which my brain has to weave a tissue of life that is comely.'

And then he foresees the day as well as he can. His experience teaches him where he will have difficulty, and he administers to his brain the lessons of which it will have most need. He carefully looks the machine over, and arranges it specially for the sort of road which he knows that it will have to traverse. And especially he readjusts his point of view, for his point of view is continually getting wrong. He is continually seeing worries where he ought to see material. He may notice, for instance, a patch on the back of his head, and he wonders whether it is the result of age or of disease, or whether it has always been there. And his wife tells him he must call at the chemist's and satisfy himself at once. Frightful nuisance! Age! The endless trouble of a capillary complaint! Calling at the chemist's will make him late at the office! etc. etc. But then his skilled, efficient brain intervenes: 'What peculiarly interesting material this mean and petty circumstance yields for the practice of philosophy and right living!' And again: 'Is *this* to ruffle you, O my soul? Will it serve any end whatever that I should buzz nervously round this circumstance instead of attending to my usual business?'

I give this as an example of the necessity of adjusting the point of view, and of the manner in which a brain habituated by suitable concentration to correct thinking will come to the rescue in unexpected contingencies. Naturally it will work with greater certainty in the manipulation of difficulties that are expected, that can be 'seen coming '; and preparation for the expected is, fortunately, preparation for the unexpected. The man who commences his day by a steady contemplation of the dangers which the next sixteen hours are likely to furnish, and by arming himself specially against those dangers, has thereby armed himself, though to a less extent, against dangers which he did not dream of. But the routine must be fairly elastic. It may be necessary to commence several days in succession—for a week or for months, even—with disciplining the brain in one particular detail, to the temporary neglect of other matters. It is astonishing how you can weed every inch of a garden path and keep it in the most meticulous order, and then one morning find in the very middle of it a lusty, full-grown plant whose roots are positively mortised in granite! All gardeners are familiar with such discoveries.

But a similar discovery, though it entails hard labour on him, will not disgust the man whose hobby is his brain. For the discovery in itself is part of the material out of which he has to live. If a man is to turn everything whatsoever into his own calm, dignity, and happiness, he must make this use even of his own failures. He must look at them as phenomena of the brain in that box, and cheerfully set about taking measures to prevent their repetition. All that happens to him, success or check, will but serve to increase his interest in the contents of that box. I seem to hear you saying: 'And a fine egotist he'll be!' Well, he'll be the right sort of egotist. The average man is not half enough of an egotist. If egotism means a terrific interest in one's self, egotism is absolutely essential to efficient living. There is no getting away from that. But if egotism means selfishness, the serious student of the craft of daily living will not be an egotist for more than about a year. In a year he will have proved the ineptitude of egotism.

XIII
SUCCESS AND FAILURE

I am sadly aware that these brief chapters will be apt to convey, especially to the trustful and enthusiastic reader, a false impression; the impression of simplicity; and that when experience has roughly corrected this impression, the said reader, unless he is most solemnly warned, may abandon the entire enterprise in a fit of disgust, and for ever afterwards maintain a cynical and impolite attitude towards all theories of controlling the human machine. Now, the enterprise is not a simple one. It is based on one simple principle—the conscious discipline of the brain by selected habits of thought—but it is just about as complicated as anything well could be. Advanced golf is child's play compared to it. The man who briefly says to himself: 'I will get up at 8, and from 8.30 to 9 I will examine and control my brain, and so my life will at once be instantly improved out of recognition'—that man is destined to unpleasant surprises. Progress will be slow. Progress may appear to be quite rapid at first, and then a period of futility may set in, and the would-be vanquisher of his brain may suffer a series of the most deadly defeats. And in his pessimism he may imagine that all his pains have gone for nothing, and that the unserious loungers in exhibition gardens and readers of novels in parlours are in the right of it after all. He may even feel rather ashamed of himself for having been, as he thinks, taken in by specious promises, like the purchaser of a quack medicine.

The conviction that great effort has been made and no progress achieved is the chief of the dangers that affront the beginner in machine-tending. It is, I will assert positively, in every case a conviction unjustified by the facts, and usually it is the mere result of reaction after fatigue, encouraged by the instinct for laziness. I do not think it will survive an impartial examination; but I know that a man, in order to find an excuse for abandoning further effort, is capable of convincing himself that past effort has yielded no fruit at all. So curious is the human machine. I beg every student of himself to consider this remark with all the intellectual honesty at his disposal. It is a grave warning.

When the machine-tender observes that he is frequently changing his point of view; when he notices that what he regarded as the kernel of the difficulty yesterday has sunk to a triviality to-day, being replaced by a fresh phenomenon; when he arises one morning and by means of a new, unexpected glimpse into the recesses of the machine perceives that hitherto he has been quite wrong and must begin again; when he wonders how on earth he could have been so blind and so stupid as not to see what now he sees; when the new vision is veiled by new disappointments and narrowed by continual reservations; when he is overwhelmed by the complexity of his undertaking—then let him unhearten himself, for he is succeeding. The history of success in any art—and machine-tending is an art—is a history of recommencements, of the dispersal and reforming of doubts, of an ever-increasing conception of the extent of the territory unconquered, and an ever-decreasing conception of the extent of the territory conquered.

It is remarkable that, though no enterprise could possibly present more diverse and changeful excitements than the mastering of the brain, the second great danger which threatens its ultimate success is nothing but a mere drying-up of enthusiasm for it! One would have thought that in an affair which concerned him so nearly, in an affair whose results might be in a very strict sense vital to him, in an affair upon which his happiness and misery might certainly turn, a man would not weary from sheer tedium. Nevertheless, it is so. Again and again I have noticed the abandonment, temporary or permanent, of this mighty and thrilling enterprise from simple lack of interest. And I imagine that, in practically all cases save those in which an exceptional original force of will renders the enterprise scarcely necessary, the interest in it will languish unless it is regularly nourished from without. Now, the interest in it cannot be nourished from without by means of conversation with other brain-tamers. There are certain things which may not be discussed by sanely organised people; and this is one. The affair is too intimate, and it is also too moral. Even after only a few minutes' vocalisation on this subject a deadly infection seems to creep into the air—the infection of priggishness. (Or am I mistaken, and do I fancy this horror? No; I cannot believe that I am mistaken.)

Hence the nourishment must be obtained by reading; a little reading every day. I suppose there are some thousands of authors who have written with more or less sincerity on the management of the human machine. But the two which, for me, stand out easily above all the rest are Marcus Aurelius Antoninus and Epictetus. Not much has been discovered since their time. 'The perfecting of life is a power residing in the soul,' wrote Marcus Aurelius in the ninth book of *To Himself*, over seventeen hundred years ago. Marcus Aurelius is assuredly regarded as the greatest of writers in the human machine school, and not to read him daily is considered by many to be a bad habit. As a confession his work stands alone. But as a practical 'Bradshaw' of existence, I would put the discourses of Epictetus before M. Aurelius. Epictetus is grosser; he will call you a blockhead as soon as look at you; he is witty, he is even humorous, and he never wanders far away from the incidents of daily life. He is brimming over with actuality for readers of the year 1908. He was a freed slave. M. Aurelius was an emperor, and he had the morbidity from which all emperors must suffer. A finer soul than Epictetus, he is not, in my view, so useful a companion. Not all of us can breathe freely in his atmosphere. Nevertheless, he is of course to be read, and re-read continually. When you have gone through Epictetus—a single page or paragraph per day, well masticated and digested, suffices—you can go through M. Aurelius, and then you can return to Epictetus, and so on, morning by morning, or night by night, till your life's end. And they will conserve your interest in yourself.

In the matter of concentration, I hesitate to recommend Mrs. Annie Besant's *Thought Power*, and yet I should be possibly unjust if I did not recommend it, having regard to its immense influence on myself. It is not one of the best books of this astounding woman. It is addressed to theosophists, and can only be completely understood in the light of theosophistic doctrines. (To grasp it all I found myself obliged to study a much larger work dealing with theosophy as a whole.) It contains an appreciable quantity of what strikes me as feeble sentimentalism, and also a lot of sheer dogma. But it is the least unsatisfactory manual of the brain that I have met with. And if the profane reader ignores all that is either Greek or twaddle to him, there will yet remain for his advantage a vast amount of very sound information and advice. All these three books are cheap.

XIV

A MAN AND HIS ENVIRONMENT

I now come to an entirely different aspect of the whole subject. Hitherto I have dealt with the human machine as a contrivance for adapting the man to his environment. My aim has been to show how much depends on the machine and how little depends on the environment, and that the essential business of the machine is to utilise, for making the stuff of life, the particular environment in which it happens to find itself—and no other! All this, however, does not imply that one must accept, fatalistically and permanently and passively, any preposterous environment into which destiny has chanced to throw us.

If we carry far enough the discipline of our brains, we can, no doubt, arrive at surprisingly good results in no matter what environment. But it would not be 'right reason' to expend an excessive amount of will-power on brain-discipline when a slighter effort in a different direction would produce consequences more felicitous. A man whom fate had pitched into a canal might accomplish miracles in the way of rendering himself amphibian; he might stagger the world by the spectacle of his philosophy under amazing difficulties; people might pay sixpence a head to come and see him; but he would be less of a nincompoop if he climbed out and arranged to live definitely on the bank.

The advantage of an adequate study of the control of the machine, such as I have outlined, is that it enables the student to judge, with some certainty, whether the unsatisfactoriness of his life is caused by a disordered machine or by an environment for which the machine is, in its fundamental construction, unsuitable. It does help him to decide justly whether, in the case of a grave difference between them, he, or the rest of the universe, is in the wrong. And also, if he decides that he is not in the wrong, it helps him to choose a new environment, or to modify the old, upon some scientific principle. The vast majority of people never know, with any precision, why they are dissatisfied with their sojourn on this planet. They make long and fatiguing excursions in search of precious materials which all the while are concealed in their own breasts. They don't know what they want; they only know that they want something. Or, if they contrive to settle in their own minds what they do want, a hundred to one the obtaining of it will leave them just as far off contentment as they were at the beginning! This is a matter of daily observation: that people are frantically engaged in attempting to get hold of things which, by universal experience, are hideously disappointing to those who have obtained possession of them. And still the struggle goes on, and probably will go on. All because brains are lying idle! 'It is no trifle that is at stake,' said Epictetus as to the question of control of instinct by reason. '*It means, Are you in your senses or are you not*?' In this significance, indubitably the vast majority of people are not in their senses; otherwise they would not behave as they do, so vaguely, so happy-go-luckily, so blindly. But the man whose brain is in working order emphatically *is* in his senses.

And when a man, by means of the efficiency of his brain, has put his reason in definite command over his instincts, he at once sees things in a truer perspective than was before possible, and therefore he is able to set a just value upon the various parts which go to make up his environment. If, for instance, he lives in London, and is aware of constant friction, he will be led to examine the claims of London as a Mecca for intelligent persons. He may say to himself: 'There is something wrong, and the seat of trouble is not in the machine. London compels me to tolerate dirt, darkness, ugliness, strain, tedious daily journeyings, and general expensiveness. What does London give me in exchange?' And he may decide that, as London offers him nothing special in exchange except the glamour of London and an occasional seat at a good concert or a bad play, he may get a better return for his expenditure of brains, nerves, and money in the provinces. He may perceive, with a certain French novelist, that 'most people of truly distinguished mind prefer the provinces.' And he may then actually, in obedience to reason, quit the deceptions of London with a tranquil heart, sure of his diagnosis. Whereas a man who had not devoted much time to the care of his mental machinery could not screw himself up to the step, partly from lack of resolution, and partly because he had never examined the sources of his unhappiness. A man who, not having full control of his machine, is consistently dissatisfied with his existence, is like a man who is being secretly poisoned and cannot decide with what or by whom. And so he has no middle course between absolute starvation and a continuance of poisoning.

As with the environment of place, so with the environment of individuals. Most friction between individuals is avoidable friction; sometimes, however, friction springs from such deep causes that no skill in the machine can do away with it. But how is the man whose brain is not in command of his existence to judge whether the unpleasantness can be cured or not, whether it arises in himself or in the other? He simply cannot judge. Whereas a man who keeps his brain for use and not for idle amusement will, when he sees that friction persists in spite of his brain, be so clearly impressed by the advisability of separation as the sole cure that he will steel himself to the effort necessary for a separation. One of the chief advantages of an efficient brain is that an efficient brain is capable of acting with firmness and resolution, partly, of course, because it has been toned up, but more because its operations are not confused by the interference of mere instincts.

Thirdly, there is the environment of one's general purpose in life, which is, I feel convinced, far more often hopelessly wrong and futile than either the environment of situation or the environment of individuals. I will be bold enough to say that quite seventy per cent. of ambition is never realised at all, and that ninety-nine per cent. of all realised ambition is fruitless. In other words, that a gigantic sacrifice of the present to the future is always going on. And here again the utility of brain-discipline is most strikingly shown. A man whose first business it is every day to concentrate his mind on the proper performance of that particular day, must necessarily conserve his interest in the present. It is impossible that his perspective should become so warped that he will devote, say, fifty-five years of his career to problematical preparations for his comfort and his glory during the final ten years. A man whose brain is his servant, and not his lady-help or his pet dog, will be in receipt of such daily content and satisfaction that he will early ask himself the question: 'As for this ambition that is eating away my hours, what will it give me that I have not already got?' Further, the steady development of interest in the hobby (call it!) of common-sense daily living will act as an automatic test of any ambition. If an ambition survives and flourishes on the top of that daily cultivation of the machine, then the owner of the ambition may be sure that it is a genuine and an invincible ambition, and he may pursue it in full faith; his developed care for the present will prevent him from making his ambition an altar on which the whole of the present is to be offered up.

I shall be told that I want to do away with ambition, and that ambition is the great motive-power of existence, and that therefore I am an enemy of society and the truth is not in me. But I do not want to do away with ambition. What I say is that current ambitions usually result in disappointment, that they usually mean the complete distortion of a life. This is an incontestable fact, and the reason of it is that ambitions are chosen either without knowledge of their real value or without knowledge of what they will cost. A disciplined brain will at once show the unnecessariness of most ambitions, and will ensure that the remainder shall be conducted with reason. It will also convince its possessor that the ambition to live strictly according to the highest common sense during the next twenty-four hours is an ambition that needs a lot of beating.

XV
L.S.D.

Anybody who really wishes to talk simple truth about money at the present time is confronted by a very serious practical difficulty. He must put himself in opposition to the overwhelming body of public opinion, and resign himself to being regarded either as a *poseur*, a crank, or a fool. The public is in search of happiness now, as it was a million years ago. Money is not the principal factor in happiness. It may be argued whether, as a factor in happiness, money is of twentieth-rate importance or fiftieth-rate importance. But it cannot be argued whether money, in point of fact, does or does not of itself bring happiness. There can be no doubt whatever that money does not bring happiness. Yet, in face of this incontrovertible and universal truth, the whole public behaves exactly as if money were the sole or the principal preliminary to happiness. The public does not reason, and it will not listen to reason; its blood is up in the money-hunt, and the philosopher might as well expostulate with an earthquake as try to take that public by the button-hole and explain. If a man sacrifices his interest under the will of some dead social tyrant in order to marry whom he wishes, if an English minister of religion declines twenty-five thousand dollars a year to go into exile and preach to New York millionaires, the phenomenon is genuinely held to be so astounding that it at once flies right round the world in the form of exclamatory newspaper articles! In an age when such an attitude towards money is sincere, it is positively dangerous—I doubt if it may not be harmful—to persist with loud obstinacy that money, instead of being the greatest, is the least thing in the world. In times of high military excitement a man may be ostracised if not lynched for uttering opinions which everybody will accept as truisms a couple of years later, and thus the wise philosopher holds his tongue—lest it should be cut out. So at the zenith of a period when the possession of money in absurd masses is an infallible means to the general respect, I have no intention either of preaching or of practising quite all that I privately in the matter of riches.

It was not always thus. Though there have been previous ages as lustful for wealth and ostentation as our own, there have also been ages when money-getting and millionaire-envying were not the sole preoccupations of the average man. And such an age will undoubtedly succeed to ours. Few things would surprise me less, in social life, than the upspringing of some anti-luxury movement, the formation of some league or guild among the middling classes (where alone intellect is to be found in quantity), the members of which would bind themselves to stand aloof from all the great, silly, banal, ugly, and tedious *luxe*-activities of the time and not to spend more than a certain sum per annum on eating, drinking, covering their bodies, and being moved about like parcels from one spot of the earth's surface to another. Such a movement would, and will, help towards the formation of an opinion which would condemn lavish expenditure on personal satisfactions as bad form. However, the shareholders of grand hotels, restaurants, and race-courses of all sorts, together with popular singers and barristers, etc., need feel no immediate alarm. The movement is not yet.

As touching the effect of money on the efficient ordering of the human machine, there is happily no necessity to inform those who have begun to interest themselves in the conduct of their own brains that money counts for very little in that paramount affair. Nothing that really helps towards perfection costs more than is within the means of every person who reads these pages. The expenses connected with daily meditation, with the building-up of mental habits, with the practice of self-control and of cheerfulness, with the enthronement of reason over the rabble of primeval instincts—these expenses are really, you know, trifling. And whether you get that well-deserved rise of a pound a week or whether you don't, you may anyhow go ahead with the machine; it isn't a motor-car, though I started by comparing it to one. And even when, having to a certain extent mastered, through sensible management of the machine, the art of achieving a daily content and dignity, you come to the embroidery of life—even the best embroidery of life is not absolutely ruinous. Meat may go up in price—it has done—but books won't. Admission to picture galleries and concerts and so forth will remain quite low. The views from Richmond Hill or Hindhead, or along Pall Mall at sunset, the smell of the earth, the taste of fruit and of kisses—these things are unaffected by the machinations of trusts and the hysteria of stock exchanges. Travel, which after books is the finest of all embroideries (and which is not to be valued by the mile but by the quality), is decidedly cheaper than ever it was. All that is required is ingenuity in one's expenditure. And much ingenuity with a little money is vastly more profitable and amusing than much money without ingenuity.

And all the while as you read this you are saying, with your impatient sneer: 'It's all very well; it's all very fine talking, *but* ...' In brief, you are not convinced. You cannot deracinate that wide-rooted dogma within your soul that more money means more joy. I regret it. But let me put one question, and let me ask you to answer it honestly. Your financial means are greater now than they used to be. Are you happier or less discontented than you used to be? Taking your existence day by day, hour by hour, judging it by the mysterious *feel* (in the chest) of responsibilities, worries, positive joys and satisfactions, are you genuinely happier than you used to be?

I do not wish to be misunderstood. The financial question cannot be ignored. If it is true that money does not bring happiness, it is no less true that the lack of money induces a state of affairs in which efficient living becomes doubly difficult. These two propositions, superficially perhaps self-contradictory, are not really so. A modest income suffices for the fullest realisation of the Ego in terms of content and dignity; but you must live within it. You cannot righteously ignore money. A man, for instance, who cultivates himself and instructs a family of daughters in everything except the ability to earn their own livelihood, and then has the impudence to die suddenly without leaving a penny—that man is a scoundrel. Ninety—or should I say ninety-nine?—per cent. of all those anxieties which render proper living almost impossible are caused by the habit of walking on the edge of one's income as one might walk on the edge of a precipice. The majority of Englishmen have some financial worry or other continually, everlastingly at the back of their minds. The sacrifice necessary to abolish this condition of things is more apparent than real. All spending is a matter of habit.

Speaking generally, a man can contrive, out of an extremely modest income, to have all that he needs—unless he needs the esteem of snobs. Habit may, and habit usually does, make it just as difficult to keep a family on two thousand a year as on two hundred. I suppose that for the majority of men the suspension of income for a single month would mean either bankruptcy, the usurer, or acute inconvenience. Impossible, under such circumstances, to be in full and independent possession of one's immortal soul! Hence I should be inclined to say that the first preliminary to a proper control of the machine is the habit of spending decidedly less than one earns or receives. The veriest automaton of a clerk ought to have the wherewithal of a whole year as a shield against the caprices of his employer. It would be as reasonable to expect the inhabitants of an unfortified city in the midst of a plain occupied by a hostile army to apply themselves successfully to the study of logarithms or metaphysics, as to expect a man without a year's income in his safe to apply himself successfully to the true art of living.

And the whole secret of relative freedom from financial anxiety lies not in income, but in expenditure. I am ashamed to utter this antique platitude. But, like most aphorisms of unassailable wisdom, it is completely ignored. You say, of course, that it is not easy to leave a margin between your expenditure and your present income. I know it. I fraternally shake your hand. Still it is, in most cases, far easier to lessen one's expenditure than to increase one's income without increasing one's expenditure. The alternative is before you. However you decide, be assured that the foundation of philosophy is a margin, and that the margin can always be had.

XVI
REASON, REASON!

In conclusion, I must insist upon several results of what I may call the 'intensive culture' of the reason. The brain will not only grow more effectively powerful in the departments of life where the brain is supposed specially to work, but it will also enlarge the circle of its activities. It will assuredly interfere in everything. The student of himself must necessarily conduct his existence more and more according to the views of his brain. This will be most salutary and agreeable both for himself and for the rest of the world. You object. You say it will be a pity when mankind refers everything to reason. You talk about the heart. You envisage an entirely reasonable existence as a harsh and callous existence.

Not so. When the reason and the heart come into conflict the heart is invariably wrong. I do not say that the reason is always entirely right, but I do say that it is always less wrong than the heart. The empire of the reason is not universal, but within its empire reason is supreme, and if other forces challenge it on its own soil they must take the consequences. Nearly always, when the heart opposes the brain, the heart is merely a pretty name which we give to our idleness and our egotism.

We pass along the Strand and see a respectable young widow standing in the gutter, with a baby in her arms and a couple of boxes of matches in one hand. We know she is a widow because of her weeds, and we know she is respectable by her clothes. We know she is not begging because she is selling matches. The sight of her in the gutter pains our heart. Our heart weeps and gives the woman a penny in exchange for a halfpenny box of matches, and the pain of our heart is thereby assuaged. Our heart has performed a good action. But later on our reason (unfortunately asleep at the moment) wakes up and says: 'That baby was hired; the weeds and matches merely a dodge. The whole affair was a spectacle got up to extract money from a fool like you. It is as mechanical as a penny in the slot. Instead of relieving distress you have simply helped to perpetuate an infamous system. You ought to know that you can't do good in that offhand way.' The heart gives pennies in the street. The brain runs the Charity Organisation Society. Of course, to give pennies in the street is much less trouble than to run the C.O.S. As a method of producing a quick, inexpensive, and pleasing effect on one's egotism the

C.O.S. is simply not in it with this dodge of giving pennies at random, without inquiry. Only—which of the two devices ought to be accused of harshness and callousness? Which of them is truly kind? I bring forward the respectable young widow as a sample case of the Heart *v.* Brain conflict. All other cases are the same. The brain is always more kind than the heart; the brain is always more willing than the heart to put itself to a great deal of trouble for a very little reward; the brain always does the difficult, unselfish thing, and the heart always does the facile, showy thing. Naturally the result of the brain's activity on society is always more advantageous than the result of the heart's activity.

Another point. I have tried to show that, if the reason is put in command of the feelings, it is impossible to assume an attitude of blame towards any person whatsoever for any act whatsoever. The habit of blaming must depart absolutely. It is no argument against this statement that it involves anarchy and the demolition of society. Even if it did (which emphatically it does not), that would not affect its truth. All great truths have been assailed on the ground that to accept them meant the end of everything. As if that mattered! As I make no claim to be the discoverer of this truth I have no hesitation in announcing it to be one of the most important truths that the world has yet to learn. However, the real reason why many people object to this truth is not because they think it involves the utter demolition of society (fear of the utter demolition of society never stopped any one from doing or believing anything, and never will), but because they say to themselves that if they can't blame they can't praise. And they do so like praising! If they are so desperately fond of praising, it is a pity that they don't praise a little more! There can be no doubt that the average man blames much more than he praises. His instinct is to blame. If he is satisfied he says nothing; if he is not, he most illogically kicks up a row. So that even if the suppression of blame involved the suppression of praise the change would certainly be a change for the better. But I can perceive no reason why the suppression of blame should involve the suppression of praise.

On the contrary, I think that the habit of praising should be fostered. (I do not suggest the occasional use of trowels, but the regular use of salt-spoons.) Anyhow, the triumph of the brain over the natural instincts (in an ideally organised man the brain and the natural instincts will never have even a tiff) always means the ultimate triumph of kindness.

And, further, the culture of the brain, the constant disciplinary exercise of the reasoning faculty, means the diminution of misdeeds. (Do not imagine I am hinting that you are on the verge of murdering your wife or breaking into your neighbour's house. Although you personally are guiltless, there is a good deal of sin still committed in your immediate vicinity.) Said Balzac in *La Cousine Bette*, 'A crime is in the first instance a defect of reasoning powers.' In the appreciation of this truth, Marcus Aurelius was, as usual, a bit beforehand with Balzac. M. Aurelius said, 'No soul wilfully misses truth.' And Epictetus had come to the same conclusion before M. Aurelius, and Plato before Epictetus. All wrong-doing is done in the sincere belief that it is the best thing to do. Whatever sin a man does he does either for his own benefit or for the benefit of society. At the moment of doing it he is convinced that it is the only thing to do. He is mistaken. And he is mistaken because his brain has been unequal to the task of reasoning the matter out. Passion (the heart) is responsible for all crimes. Indeed, crime is simply a convenient monosyllable which we apply to what happens when the brain and the heart come into conflict and the brain is defeated. That transaction of the matches was a crime, you know.

Lastly, the culture of the brain must result in the habit of originally examining all the phenomena of life and conduct, to see what they really are, and to what they lead. The heart hates progress, because the dear old thing always wants to do as has always been done. The heart is convinced that custom is a virtue. The heart of the dirty working man rebels when the State insists that he shall be clean, for no other reason than that it is his custom to be dirty. Useless to tell his heart that, clean, he will live longer! He has been dirty and he will be. The brain alone is the enemy of prejudice and precedent, which alone are the enemies of progress. And this habit of originally examining phenomena is perhaps the greatest factor that goes to the making of personal dignity; for it fosters reliance on one's self and courage to accept the consequences of the act of reasoning. Reason is the basis of personal dignity.

I finish. I have said nothing of the modifications which the constant use of the brain will bring about in the *general value of existence.* Modifications slow and subtle, but tremendous! The persevering will discover them. It will happen to the persevering that their whole lives are changed—texture and colour, too! Naught will happen to those who do not persevere.

THE END